ALL
ABOUT
DINOSAURS

Fife Council Education Department

King's Road Primary School

King's Crescent, Rosyth KY11 2RS

KINGFISHER
Kingfisher Publications Plc
New Penderel House
283-288 High Holborn
London WC1V 7HZ

First published in paperback in 1992 by Kingfisher Publications Plc
10 9 8 7
Originally published in hardback in 1990 by Kingfisher Publications Plc

BRITISH LIBRARY CATALOGUING IN PUBLICATION DATA
A catalogue record for this book is
available from the British Library

ISBN 0 86272 649 2

Edited by Camilla Hallinan
Designed by Ben White
Phototypeset by Rowland Phototypesetting Ltd,
Bury St Edmunds, Suffolk
Colour separations by Scantrans Pte Ltd, Singapore
Printed in Spain

MIKE BENTON

ALL ABOUT DINOSAURS

Illustrated by
Ann Winterbotham

Kingfisher Books

Contents

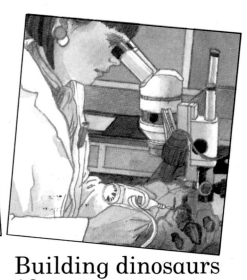

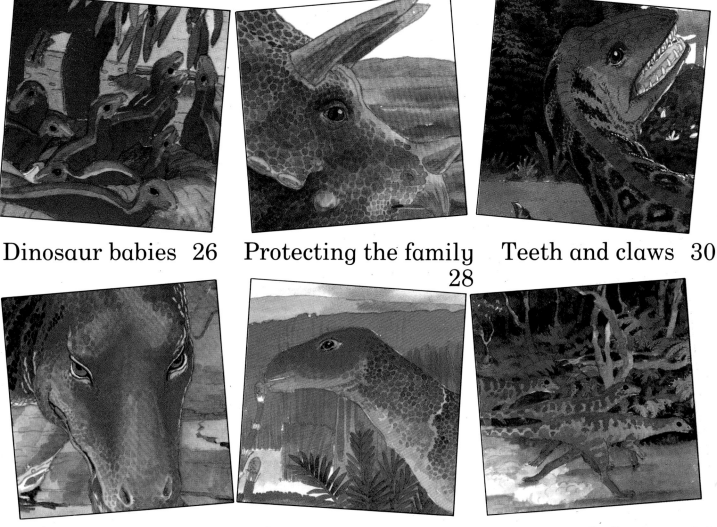

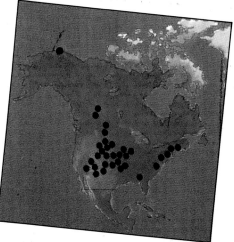

Museum monsters

Most museums have some bones of giant animals called dinosaurs. Many have whole skeletons – all the bones of the arms, legs, back, head and tail.

The word dinosaur means 'terrible reptile'. Dinosaurs lived on Earth a long time ago. There is none alive today.

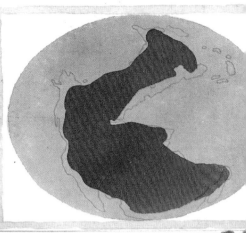

The first giants

Coelophysis

The first dinosaurs were animals such as
Coelophysis (pronounced SEE-loh-FY-sis) and
Plateosaurus (PLAT-ee-oh-SAW-rus). They lived
on Earth 220 million years ago.

Plateosaurus

When the dinosaurs were alive, the Earth did not
look the same as it does today. Two hundred and
twenty million years ago, there were different
plants, different animals and no people.

How big?

Most dinosaurs were large.
Apatosaurus (a-PAT-oh-SAW-rus)
was 21 metres long, which is
the length of three coaches
parked nose to tail. It was
tall enough to look through
a window on the second floor!

Other dinosaurs were smaller,
the size of rhinos and elephants.

One or two were really small,
just the size of a hen.

Can you find these dinosaurs?
  Apatosaurus
  Compsognathus
    (komp-SOG-na-thus)
  Struthiomimus
    (STROOTH-ee-oh-MY-mus)
  Iguanodon (ig-WA-noh-don)
  Stegosaurus (STEG-oh-SAW-rus)
  Triceratops (try-SER-a-tops)

Stegosaurus

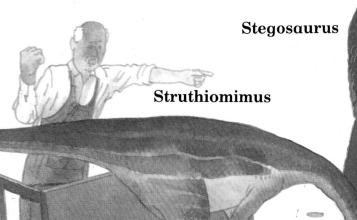

Struthiomimus

Apatosaurus

Iguanodon

Triceratops

Compsognathus

13

Record-breakers

Which were the largest and smallest dinosaurs?

Compsognathus (komp-SOG-na-thus) is the smallest dinosaur we know. It was only 60 centimetres long from its head to its tail. Its body was the same size as a hen. Can you see Compsognathus on the other page?

Of course, baby dinosaurs were even smaller. Mussaurus (muss-AW-rus) was no bigger than a kitten. Psittacosaurus (SI-tak-oh-SAW-rus) was just the size of a pigeon.

Psittacosaurus

Mussaurus

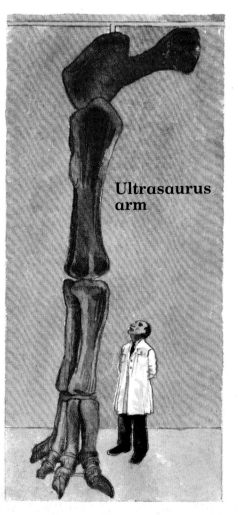

Ultrasaurus arm

For a long time, scientists thought that the biggest dinosaur was Brachiosaurus (BRACK-ee-oh-SAW-rus). It was over 20 metres long and weighed between 70 and 80 tonnes. But in 1979 a giant arm was found . . . Now scientists think that there were even bigger dinosaurs, which we call Ultrasaurus (ultra-SAW-rus) and Supersaurus (super-SAW-rus).

It is hard to work out how big these dinosaurs were because only some of their bones have been found. But we can guess that Ultrasaurus may have been 30 metres long and weighed 130 tonnes. That is as heavy as 25 elephants!

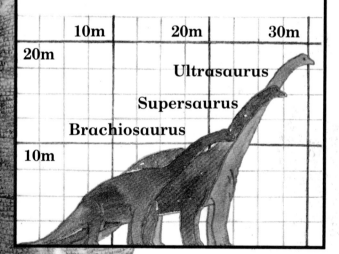

	10m		20m		30m
20m					
				Ultrasaurus	
				Supersaurus	
			Brachiosaurus		
10m					

Finding fossils

Dinosaur bones have been found all over the world. Digging up a dinosaur is hard work, because the bones are covered in rock and are fossilized. (Fossils are the remains of animals and plants that died a long time ago. They are preserved in rock.)

When some bones are found, a team of scientists from a museum come out to the site. Scientists who study fossils are called palaeontologists (PAL-ee-on-TOL-oh-jists).

To excavate the bones, the collectors carefully chip away the rock with chisels and fine needles. They also take photographs and draw maps of where each bone was found.

Fossils are brittle and easily broken. So the collectors cover the bones with strips of sacking soaked in wet plaster. As it dries, the plaster becomes hard and protects the bones.

The collectors label the bones and load them into a truck which carries them from the site to the museum. If the museum is far away, the bones may go by ship or by plane.

Building dinosaurs

In the museum's laboratory, technicians take the plaster off the bones with small electric saws and needles.

Then the technicians clean the bones carefully, often with a small drill under a microscope, and coat them with varnish.

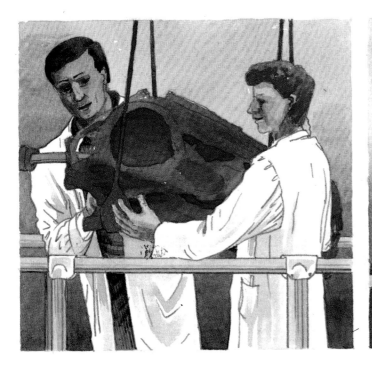

After cleaning, the bones are put together as a skeleton. They have to be held in place with a metal frame.

Sometimes an artist makes a model, to show what the dinosaur looked like when it was alive.

Now the dinosaur is ready to go on show. Twenty people have spent three years finding and rebuilding this Diplodocus (di-PLOD-oh-kus).

Dinosaur clues

Fossils give us clues about dinosaurs.

Pachycephalosaurus (PAK-ee-KEF-al-oh-SAW-rus) means 'thick-headed reptile'. Its skull has a high dome of thick bone. Why?

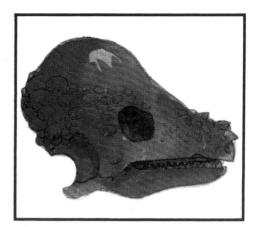

Many animals fight for territory and mates. Sheep have thick-boned skulls to protect the brain during a fight. Perhaps Pachycephalosaurus had a dome for the same reason, to protect its brain during a head-on clash.

Male and female

Male and female animals of the
same species sometimes look
different, in size or shape or
colour. It was probably the
same with dinosaurs.

Fossils of the duck-billed
dinosaurs show that the male
and female had different head
shapes.

Parasaurolophus (pa-ra-SAW-roh-LOH-fus)
had an amazing crest on its head. The males
had much larger ones than the females.

Sometimes young animals look different from the adults.

young Corythosaurus

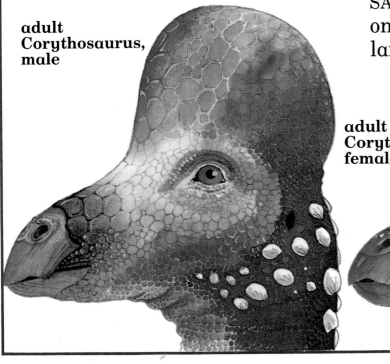

adult Corythosaurus, male

Another duck-billed dinosaur, Corythosaurus (ko-RITH-oh-SAW-rus), had a small crest on its head. This became larger as it grew up.

adult Corythosaurus, female

But there are some things which fossils can't tell us. What colours were the dinosaurs? What noises did they make? How did they behave? We often have to guess the answer to these questions by looking at the way animals live today.

Nests and eggs

Dinosaurs laid eggs, just as reptiles and birds do today. We know a lot about dinosaur eggs from finds of Maiasaura (MY-a-SAW-ra), a duck-billed dinosaur. Maiasaura means 'good mother reptile'!

The mother dug a large round hollow in the sand and made it into a nest. Then she laid 20 or 30 eggs, and covered them with leaves to keep them warm.

Alligators are reptiles that cover their nests too; the leaves keep their eggs warm until the babies hatch out.

Maiasaura may also have sat on her nest, to keep her eggs warm. Many birds incubate their eggs in the same way.

A hen sits on her eggs for about 21 days. Then the chicks hatch. Maiasaura laid bigger eggs. So she must have sat on her nest for at least 30 days.

Palaeontologists have found fossil eggs with baby dinosaurs inside. The fossils show that each baby grew to a length of between 40 and 50 centimetres before it hatched out.

Dinosaur babies

The newborn Maiasaura (MY-a-SAW-ra) babies
were small and helpless. Their parents must have
protected them from hungry meat-eaters.
They probably fed them with leaves too.

The babies grew very quickly. After a year
they were perhaps three or four times bigger.
By the age of four or five, Maiasaura was
grown up.

Protecting the family

The bones of many Triceratops (try-SER-a-tops) have been found together, so palaeontologists think that they lived in large family groups, like herds of elephants, grazing on plants.

Triceratops was nine metres long and weighed over five tonnes.

The adults could have protected their young from dangerous dinosaurs by making a circle around them.

Triceratops had a pointed horn on its snout, just like a rhinoceros, and two horns over its eyes. If Tyrannosaurus (tie-RAN-oh-SAW-rus) tried to attack, Triceratops lowered its head and swung its great horns. The bony frill at the back of the head protected its neck from Tyrannosaurus's teeth and claws.

Teeth and claws

How do we know which dinosaurs ate meat and which fed on plants? Fossils of their teeth and claws give us clues.

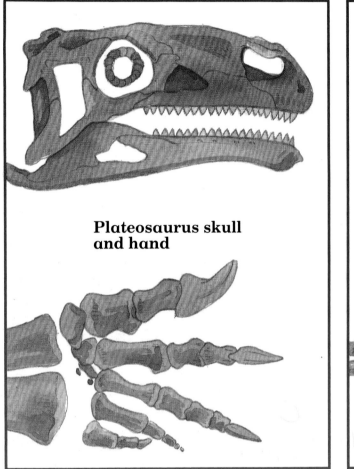

Plateosaurus skull and hand

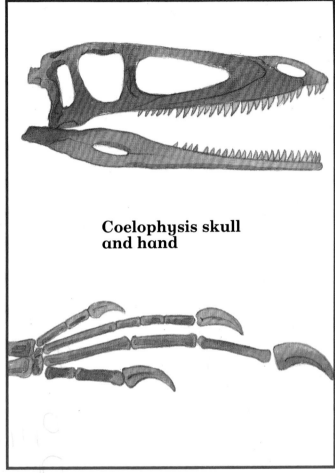

Coelophysis skull and hand

Some dinosaurs, such as Plateosaurus (PLAT-ee-oh-SAW-rus), had small pointed teeth to munch leaves and twigs.

Plant-eaters had broad hands with short fingers and claws for pulling in leaves.

Other dinosaurs, such as Coelophysis (SEE-loh-FY-sis), had long curved teeth with sharp edges for cutting meat.

Meat-eaters also had strong claws on their long fingers, which they used to grip their prey.

One of the fiercest meat-eaters was Deinonychus (DIE-noh-NY-kus). When it hunted its prey, it kicked out with its feet, which had an enormous slashing claw. Then Deinonychus tore flesh off with its hands and teeth.

A meat-eater

Tyrannosaurus rex (tie-RAN-oh-SAW-rus REKS) means 'king tyrant reptile'. It was the most terrifying of the meat-eating dinosaurs, with teeth each as long as a table knife.

Tyrannosaurus was 15 metres long and more than five metres tall. It used its massive feet to hold down its prey and stripped away flesh with its massive teeth. Tyrannosaurus could have eaten you whole!

A vegetarian

Iguanodon (ig-WA-noh-don) lived in herds and fed on plants. It pulled the leaves into its mouth with a long tongue, just as a giraffe does today, and ground them up with broad blunt teeth.

Iguanodon was ten metres long, and five metres high when it stood on its hind legs.

Iguanodon was one of the first dinosaurs to be found, in 1822. Scientists at the time thought that Iguanodon was like a rhinoceros, with a horn on its nose. But we now know that the 'horn' is actually a spike on its thumb!

Dinosaur defences

Iguanodon (ig-WA-noh-don) may have used the bony spike on its thumb to fight off meat-eaters.

Other big plant-eaters, such as this Apatosaurus (a-PAT-oh-SAW-rus), also had long claws to defend themselves against attack.

Diplodocus (di-PLOD-oh-kus) was the longest plant-eater, 27 metres from nose to tail!

If it was attacked, Diplodocus could lash its long thin tail from side to side like a whip.

Small dinosaurs could just run away from big meat-eaters.

Hypsilophodon (hip-sih-LOFF-oh-don) could run at 40 kilometres per hour, about as fast as a racehorse!

Scientists can work out how fast a dinosaur ran by looking at its skeleton and at its footprints fossilized in rock.

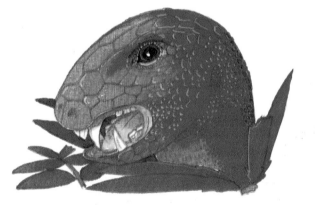

Some small plant-eaters had fangs. Heterodontosaurus (HET-er-oh-DONT-oh-SAW-rus) may have used these to bite its attacker.

Other dinosaurs had a thick layer of bony skin which protected them like a suit of armour.

Hylaeosaurus (HY-lee-oh-SAW-rus) crouched down so that a meat-eater couldn't get under its armour.

Armour

Ankylosaurus (an-KY-low-SAW-rus) was six metres long and with its heavy armour it weighed ten tonnes or more. When it ran at speed, Ankylosaurus must have looked like a tank or a bulldozer!

Ankylosaurus was a plant-eater which fed peacefully on leaves from low bushes.

But when it was attacked by Tyrannosaurus (tie-RAN-oh-SAW-rus), Ankylosaurus crouched down and swung its heavy tail like a club, with great force.

A dinosaur mystery

Stegosaurus (STEG-oh-SAW-rus), which means 'roofed reptile', had a row of bony plates along the middle of its back. What were these plates used for?

Perhaps the plates were used in defence. They may have helped to protect Stegosaurus from attacks by a meat-eater such as this big Allosaurus (AL-oh-SAW-rus).

Perhaps the plates helped Stegosaurus to control its body temperature, by taking in the sun's heat when it was cold and letting out heat to cool down when it was hot.

What happened?

Sixty-six million years ago, the dinosaurs died out. We are not sure why this happened.

At one time, scientists thought that the early mammals ate the dinosaurs' eggs. But dinosaurs laid lots of eggs and their eggs were big. So how could those little mammals have eaten all of the eggs?

Another idea is that the weather got colder and the dinosaurs could not survive through the icy winters. But this change of climate may have taken thousands or millions of years. So why didn't the dinosaurs get used to the cold?

Some scientists think that a giant meteorite ten kilometres wide fell from space and hit our planet. The great explosion sent clouds of dust around the Earth and many animals died out within a few days.

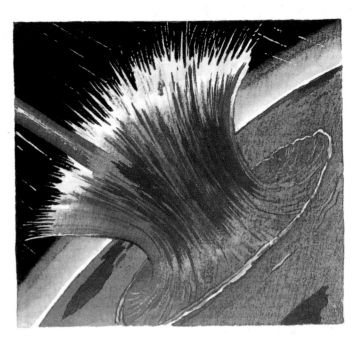

But crocodiles, frogs, birds and mammals did not die out. These animals are still here today.

No one knows which is the right answer.

Where to see dinosaurs

The dots on this map show sites where
dinosaur fossils have been found. Scientists
are still looking for more, all over the world.

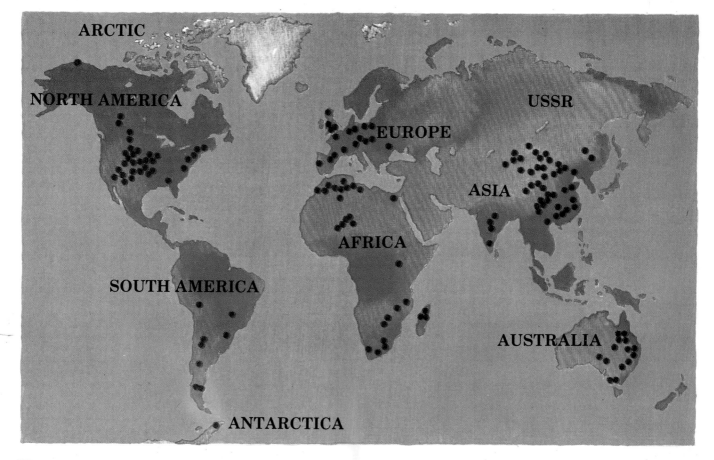

You can go and see a dinosaur in these museums:

**Birmingham Museum and
Art Gallery** Natural History)
Chamberlain Square
Birmingham B3 3DH

The Dinosaur Museum
Icen Way
Dorchester
Dorset DT1 1EW

Hunterian Museum
The University
Glasgow G12 8QQ

The Leicestershire Museums
96 New Walk
Leicester LE1 6TD

Museum of Isle of Wight Geology
Sandown Library
High Street
Sandown
Isle of Wight PO36 8AF

National Museum of Wales
Cathays Park
Cardiff CF1 1XL

The Natural History Museum
Cromwell Road
London SW7 5BD

The Royal Museum of Scotland
Chambers Street
Edinburgh EH1 1JF

Sedgwick Museum
Cambridge University
Downing Street
Cambridge CB2 3EQ

Ulster Museum
Botanic Gardens
Belfast BT9 5AB

University Museum
Parks Road
Oxford OX1 3PW

Index